DEDICATION

This book is dedicated to Cecilia. You are my greatest love.

TABLE OF CONTENTS

Chapter 1- The Do-Now Tips to Fast-Track Profits............................ 5

Chapter 2- Converting Your Website into a Money-Making Machine 9

Chapter 3- Create Your Own Products 18

Chapter 4- Earn Cash Selling Your Talents to Someone Else 27

Chapter 5- Blog about What You Love 39

Chapter 6- Other Tips to Earn If You Have no Writing/Design Talents 43

Chapter 7- Habits to Form to Telecommute Successfully 53

Chapter 8- Other Means to Earn without Borrowing.....................60

About The Author...67

CHAPTER 1- THE DO-NOW TIPS TO FAST-TRACK PROFITS

Does the idea of working online and earning money from the comfort of your own home sound appealing to you? More people are taking advantage of the wonderful opportunities online to earn their own money and be their own boss while not having to leave their home. Working from home can be fun and easy. In as little as 30 days you can begin earning a profit from your online business.

Ever since the internet became part of our daily lives, internet businesses have been popping up all over the net. The convenience of the internet cannot be too understated. It allows people to communicate with those all over the world with a click of the mouse. It can enable people to have business meetings without leaving the office. It can also allow someone to work from home.

Say No to Shark Lenders!

More people in the work force are working from home as it is not always necessary to go into the office. Still others are deciding to branch out on their own and create their own businesses online.

Anyone can make a living working from online at home. You just have to know what talents you do have and how to direct those talents. If you have a computer, you can use it to play games and e-mail friends, or you can use it to work for you. It is your choice. If you want to have your own business, be your own boss and work from the comfort of your own home, you can do so online.

Imagine getting up in the morning whenever you please, making a cup of coffee and heading to the office which is located in your home - still wearing your pajamas! More people are doing this each year. Imagine being your own boss and not having to answer to anyone but yourself and your customers. Imagine having no limit on to what you can make if you want to work hard.

The dream of working online from your home can easily become a reality if you follow the simple instructions in this guide. Here you will learn all about the different ways that anyone can make money by working online from their home, no matter what sort of skills they have or do not have.

Working from home online and earning money should be viewed as the same as any other business that you begin on your own. You must keep accurate records and be disciplined. Realize that it takes time to get started and build up your business online. You can continue to work at your outside job when getting started, but in order for you to succeed and make real money, you will have to treat your online money making business as a full time job. That means that if you like to sleep late, you will need to also stay up late and work in order to succeed.

If you have the time and determination, you can be successful at making money online from your own home, no matter what your skills or talents. If you are not self-disciplined and fear that you may end up wasting time and not working when you are at home, do not worry. This is something that can be taught and you will receive some tips on working from home in this book. The only thing you need to be successful and work from home online is a computer, a willingness to learn new concepts and steely determination. If you have those, you are ready to begin your new exciting career on the fast track to making money online from home!

How Do You Begin Fast-Tracking Your Profits Online?

The first thing you need to do is to figure out what you know how to do and what you would like to do with your time online. Do you have any specific talents? Are you tech savvy and understand how to set up a website? Do you enjoy selling products and have a bit of money to spend for stock? Do you like to write or film videos? Do you have absolutely no talent but still want to make money? No matter what your answer to the aforementioned questions, as long as you have a computer that works, you can make money online.

Your individual talents, or lack of talents, will determine what you can do online. No matter what type of talent you have or do not have, if you have a computer, you can learn to make money online from the comfort of your home. Take stock of what you have and make sure that your computer is in good working order. From now on, your computer is no longer an electronic instrument in your home, but your business partner. Make sure that you take care of it as you will become dependent upon this piece of technology to earn a living.

One of the first things you will want to do prior to starting your business is open a PayPal account. Many online businesses pay

Say No to Shark Lenders!

through PayPal or similar online banking options. PayPal is an easy account to open. You can link it with your bank account or credit card and easily receive payments to your account. If you apply for the PayPal Debit Card, you can use it as a credit card when shopping and receive a rebate back for every purchase. You can also transfer funds from your PayPal account to your bank account free of charge. There are other online services such as PayPal, but for the current time, PayPal is the most popular.

Do not be afraid of opening a PayPal account. Contrary to popular belief, it is not risky and the site is very secure. You will be required to provide certain information, including credit or debit card information and your bank information and then verify that this information is accurate. This can take several days before you are certified so you should start this process as soon as you know that you are going to open a business. There is no charge to open a PayPal account.

Once you have opened a PayPal account, you can get started making money online from the comfort of your home. You just have to decide what it is that you want to do.

Chapter 2 - Converting Your Website into a Money-Making Machine

Most people who are successful at making money online have their own website. A website is not like a web page, like a Myspace page. It is an entire site that needs a domain name, a server and must be set up either using software designed to create a website or by someone who knows how to create a website online. Website design is an art specialty and many people go to school to learn this skill. We will be talking about how people who know how to design websites can make money online later in this book, but for now, suffice to say that if you really want to make big money, you will get your own website.

There are many different things that you can do with your website. You can sell products from your website, you can host ads, and you can even become an affiliate for one of the many online marketing companies. No matter what you plan to do online, chances are that you will need a website.

Say No to Shark Lenders!

Because there are so many opportunities for anyone who has their own website online, it may help you to learn how to create your own website, how to register a domain name and how to find a server to host your website. Once you learn how to create your own website, there is no limit as to the number of websites that you can create and collect money from. We will begin talking about how you can make money on your website in the next chapter.

If you have a friend who knows how to create websites, you may be able to form a partnership with him or her and split any profits you make on your website business with your partner. This may be cheaper than hiring someone to create the website for you.

You will want to make sure that you create an independent website where you are free to post ads of your own and also sell whatever you like. There are many places online that offer a low rate to host a website for individuals and give you the templates you need to create the website. While these types of websites may be ideal for family style websites, they are not advisable for those who want to make money off of advertising on their website as they usually prohibit ads. If you think you are going to make money off of your Yahoo sponsored website, think again. You are going to need to get your own website and your own server in order to be able to sponsor ads and products.

You do not have to worry about what to put on your website. Not yet. Content is easy to find and plentiful online. You can also create your own content quite easily. You just want to get your website up and going, have your PayPal account ready and then you will be in the position to begin making money online from the comfort of your own home.

Earn as an Affiliate

If you have a website, you can make some money from commission sales by becoming an affiliate of one of the many online marketing companies that represent certain products. The products are advertised on your website and when people purchase these online products or services, you get a percentage of the profit.

How does this work? Let us use auto insurance for an example. You become an affiliate of a marketing company that advertises ABC Auto Insurance Company. ABC Auto Insurance Company logos and ads appear on your website and every time someone who clicks on your website clicks on the ad and purchases ABC Auto Insurance, you get a percentage of the sales commission. In some cases, percentages are as high as 25 percent. And you are not limited only to ABC Auto Insurance. You can also advertise other online products on your website. And every time someone purchases one of these internet products or services, you get a cut of the profit.

It does sound easy. It is very simple. It costs nothing to become an affiliate, you need only sign up and wait for the profits to be deposited into your PayPal account. Most of these online marketing companies pay directly once a month through PayPal. The trick is attracting people to your website. The only way to do this is to have some sort of content on your website that will attract visitors. But you do not want just any visitors to your website. You want visitors who want to purchase car insurance and the other products for which you get a commission. Becoming an affiliate is easy. Getting traffic to your website is a whole different ball game.

You need to attract people to your website who may be customers of ABC Auto Insurance. Therefore, you need content that will be picked up in the search engines that will appeal to people who may purchase ABC Auto Insurance. Find out about ABC Auto Insurance. Is it a discount rate insurance company that panders to young people? If that is the case, you can put stock your website with content that will attract young men and women who may be in the market for cheap auto insurance.

You can use videos, photos, music and text on your website to attract traffic to your website. Videos are becoming more popular and humorous videos are often shown on sites like "You Tube" and other internet video sharing sites. A funny video that has something that would attract young people can be placed on "You Tube" with a blurb about your site. This is but one way to attract potential customers of ABC Auto Insurance to your website.

An even better way is to put SEO text in your website designed to attract people who want to purchase auto insurance. SEO stands for search engine optimized. This means that you will use certain keywords that people, when searching through the internet for information, will pick up in the search engines. You can have several articles on your website that use the words "discount auto insurance" throughout the article so that when someone does a search for "discount auto insurance" your website pops up. They click on your website and peruse your article, and with any luck, they click on the ad for ABC Auto Insurance and sign up. Then you get a commission. Of course, it will take more than one SEO article about auto insurance and more than one visitor to your website to get you on the track of making money, but you get the idea.

We will talk about promoting your website later in this book. For now, let it suffice that you should have articles on your website that pertain to the products of which you are an affiliate. If you cannot write your own SEO articles for your website, there are plenty of writers online who will be glad to write for your website.

You can offer to pay for their articles upfront or you can promise them a percentage of any profits that you make.

Becoming an affiliate for an online marketing site is easy, free and is an ideal way to make money online from the comfort of your home. The only thing you need is a website with some content. Once you have the ads, you can continue to add to your content and promote your website to people who will be interested in the products you are pandering

Get Rich through Website Ads

Most people online have seen ads on different websites. These ads are placed in strategic places and on websites where they have some sort of relevance. You can sign up with AdSense for free and Google will place ads on your website that are appropriate to the content you have on your website. Each time someone clicks on the ads, you make money. Each month, Google will deposit money into your PayPal account depending on how many people clicked on the ads.

Using AdSense or other online ad companies on your website is a bit different than being an affiliate of an online marketing site. For one thing, you do not have any direct control over the ads that appear on your site. Google uses a program designed to search for key words in your content to decide which ads to place on your website. For example, if your site is all about Aromatherapy, then your google ads will most likely be for different products that pertain to Aromatherapy products and other alternate therapy and new age products.

Again, the trick to making money off of AdSense or any other online company that places ads on your website and gives you money for each time they are clicked on is to get traffic to your website. Your website content can continue to change. You can use SEO articles to drive traffic from the search engines to your site. Most people who opt to make money off of ads on their websites generally like to specialize in a particular subject matter.

There is nothing stopping you from being an affiliate and using ads on your website. You are best not to put all of your eggs in one basket. However, if you plan to be successful with making money off of your website from ads and commissions, you are best to update your website often with fresh SEO articles and specialize in a certain product or area.

AdSense is only one online company that offers money for website owners who host their ads. There are many others out there that will do the same. Getting the ads and the affiliate programs is easy. Your job will be promoting your website and increasing traffic. You will not make any money on ads or commission sales if you do not have anyone coming to your website.

How to Promote Your Website

There are many different ways to promote a website. In order to properly promote your website, you have to figure out what type of people would enjoy visiting your website and will be interested in your ads and products that you are selling. If, for example, you have a website that is all about Aromatherapy, you must figure out the demographics of the type of people who would be interested in this healing art. Chances are that they will be mostly young women.

You can then go to different sites where young women hang out on the internet. You can try some of the alternative healing sites and peruse the forums. Many websites have forums where you can post links or information. Learn where your potential customers are and start showing up. Tell them about your website and your services and, if possible, post a link to your website. Searching out potential customers and posting information on forums is but one way to increase traffic to your website.

Yet another way to promote your website is by using free social gathering websites, such as Myspace and Facebook to talk about your website and post links to the website after you have told everyone all of the benefits. This is not the time to be shy. Make sure that you take advantage of all of the social websites on the internet and try to make as many online friends as possible. Invite these people to visit your website if they want to learn more about aromatherapy, or whatever is the topic of your website. Many social websites also have forums where you can post links to your website as well. Be friendly and make sure that you make as many friends as possible to draw to your website.

Chances are that you have dozens of people in your e-mail address book. Each time you post a new SEO article on your website, make sure that you send out a link to everyone in your e-mail address book and ask them to pass the information to their friends. Never underestimate the power of word of mouth. Many of your internet friends will be glad to pass on the information to their friends if you ask them.

The best way to promote your website, however, is to continue to maintain attractive content that pertains to the ads and products of your website by using a constant influx of SEO articles. This is the best way for your website to be discovered in the search engines and will give you maximum exposure on the internet.

Leave no stone unturned whenever trying to promote your website online. Remember that the more traffic you generate towards your website, the more money you will make from the ads and possible

Say No to Shark Lenders!

sales of any products for which you are an affiliate. Use all avenues open to you to continue to promote so that you can continue to make money online while working from your home.

What If You Have No Website?

An acquaintance of mine knows an apothecary who made a skin care product. The product is distributed across the country through independent distributors. My acquaintance told me to check over the site to see if it was a product I'd be interested in trying out.

When I got to the site, I instantly forgot about why I was supposed to be viewing the web site. How come? The grammar, artwork and layout were atrocious; particularly the grammar! I rewrote the home page and sent it off to the webmaster with a courteous note stating that I'd be happy to remake the entire site for $x. Inside a few days we came to terms and I got the job. You are able to do this also.

Professionals are a good target market for freelancers. Mortgage companies, insurance companies, lawn care suppliers, and so forth. Most have sites – and a lot of them are not very good. So, edit/re-script a page and send it to them with a proposition to do the whole web site. Commonly, if they use you once, they'll continue to do so for years to come. Offer to add each week, each month, every quarter, and etcetera. Add articles to the site to step-up traffic. A lot of small business owners are so busy that they don't think or understand how to do this type of marketing. Call attention to the advantages and watch your customer list grow.

Consider the content for each page. For instance, you are able to go into company history on the "About Us" page, but you can likewise mention that your company has x years of experience on the home page, also. You are able to bullet your services on the home page and then go into detail about them on the "Services" page. Jot down some points for the content of each page. Decide where you want particular tidbits to be highlighted so each page isn't repetitious.

Add a little SEO. Do some research on the net to determine what keywords are "red-hot" for the industry. If the company, for instance, makes kitchen cabinets, you might want to include terms like "kitchen remodeling" "kitchen cabinets" and "kitchen cabinetry" to name some. It's likewise a good idea to provide a regional aspect for individuals seeking the business locally. For instance, "kitchen cabinet maker in AZ" and "kitchen cabinets AZ" are good terms to work into the copy.

Utilize an attention-grabbing headline for each page. Rather than "Cabinet Makers" you may try something like "Distinctive Cabinets for Custom Kitchens." When you get into the "core," remember to talk to your specified audience. Will you refer to the customer directly? No one truly cares about the content unless it offers them something. Rather than bragging about why the company is the best, or presenting a history of kitchen cabinets it's beneficial to keep in mind that you need to explain the advantages of what the company has to offer. What can Joe Blow get out of the site, and why should he pick this company to build his cabinets?

I always end each page with an easy "call to action." For instance, "Are you ready to discover how you are able to have the kitchen of your dreams? Contact us at (phone) or email us at (e-mail)." You get the idea. The goal is to drive the reader to take action.

CHAPTER 3- CREATE YOUR OWN PRODUCTS

If you have anything to sell on your website, do not hesitate to use your website as an online store to sell products relating to those discussed on your website. Remember we talked about a website that focuses about Aromatherapy. Suppose, in addition to procuring ads and becoming an affiliate for online marketing companies you also decide to sell your own home made Aromatherapy products or products purchased in bulk that you can sell individually online at a profit?

You can give your customers the opportunity to pay for the products by PayPal. Setting up a secure order form is not difficult for a person who understands how to design a website. Your website will consist of many different pages, all discussing the benefits of Aromatherapy and the different ways you can use it to heal. Then you can have a tab for a store where people can order products.

Now, in addition to earning a percentage of the profits from your affiliate programs and every time someone clicks on the ads on your website, you can also earn a profit from anything you decide to sell. By combining marketing, advertising and your own products, you can really put your website to work for you. Of course, you will still have to work diligently to continue to maintain the site and draw additional traffic using some of the means discussed in the last chapter.

A Little Story for Inspiration

Linda had a mortgage and two children to support when she was downsized from her job at a large corporation. She had little money put aside and had no idea what she was going to do. It seemed as though the jobs in her field were few and far between.

Linda had been paying a good portion of her income to the daycare center to care for her children when she was at work. Her ex-husband also contributed to the care as well as the day care expenses. Linda missed the days when she was able to stay home with her children and, more than anything, longed to work from home so she could spend more time with her children.

A friend told her about AdSense and how she was making money from people clicking on the ads on her website. She suggested to Linda that she do the same thing to earn a few extra bucks until she got a job. Linda had no idea what type of website she wanted to begin. Her friend suggested that she begin with something in which she had an interest. Linda always liked Rock and Roll when she was younger and noticed that a lot of the younger people were now

Say No to Shark Lenders!

interested in what they now called "Classic Rock." She decided to have a website devoted to Classic Rock.

Linda was lucky. Her friend was able to set up the website for her for free and showed Linda how to make changes and add content. Then she suggested that Linda start adding content so that she could attract people to the website.

Using videos that she uploaded from You Tube the depicted Classic Rock artists, Linda began to fill her website with videos and content about her favorite classic rock bands. She became an affiliate for an online marketing company that sold, of all things, auto insurance and a discount rate. This appealed to young people. Because she quickly learned how to write SEO articles, ads began appearing on her website for CDs, books and other items relating to rock stars. Before she knew it, Linda was earning a little bit of money from the ads and the online marketing companies of which she was an affiliate.

Linda used Myspace and other places where young people hung out on the internet to promote her site. Before long, she had a forum of her own incorporated on her website where young people congregated to talk about their favorite classic rock bands. In addition to young people, older people also began to visit the site.

An opportunity presented itself to Linda to purchase some vintage style Rock T-Shirts. Linda was a bit hesitant about investing any money into her new venture, but, once again, her friend talked her into it. After six months, Linda was glad that she began selling the T-Shirts. She stopped looking for another job and although she continued to promote her website and increase the content and sales, she had more time to spend with her children, was able to work from her home and make money online.

Linda is just one of many individuals who took the fast track to success and decided to become their own boss and make money from their homes by working online. Using a website to make money through affiliate programs, ads and even by selling merchandise is just one way that you, like Linda, can achieve financial independence from the privacy of your own home by working online.

Write Your Own Ebook

Authoring e-books is simple – it may be done in as little as twenty-four hours – and you can offer it for sale on a web site like Click Bank or Commission Junction. Think though, most individuals look to the net for info. And, "how to" info is among the most popular forms.

So, squeeze your brain for what you like to do, author an e-book about it and sell it thru a major distributor like Click Bank. One book likely won't make you rich, but it may bring in extra cash for a long time to come. The most beneficial part about this idea, once you make one e-book, you are able to make others and truly build your income to the point where you are able to quit your awful day job.

Think about your target audience, your book's advantages to them, its core, and center like a laser on that. It might seem to you that just everybody' will want to read your book - but that idea may make your book too 'generalized'. Remember, if you center your efforts on a particular topic instead of generalizing you'll appeal powerfully to a certain audience and reap more possible sales. It's rather like centering on a puddle rather than an ocean.

Get to Understand your target readers; what troubles might your book resolve for them? Where is your book purchasing audience?

Say No to Shark Lenders!
Try to author a title that includes your audience in it. If not there, then maybe in the sub-title?

You have to be author and promoter, so write and make your sales info about your book as you author your book. Collect data about yourself for your author blurb (whatever qualifies you to author the book, maybe other publishing credits, any experience that's a plus), write about the advantages your potential purchasers are seeking and are likely to discover in your book. Get a few testimonials.

Check into places like Amazon to see what books are selling well and read their 'blurb' content for thoughts on how to present your own. A visit to your local bookshop is a great idea also. Check into some of the other marketers who are marketing books online. Do an 'E-book' search. How are they marketing?

Author an attention-getting table of contents for your book. Title your chapter and add a sub-title to make it transparent to your reader what is contained inside. Read the table of contents of other authors to get an approximation of what may be 'attention-getting'.

That should get you going. Now, do some net searches, hunt down the needed info to get yourself set in motion, but mind the rip-off artist out to get your money. Subscribe to a few newsletters by individuals who are legit. Think about each step of the process, keep notes and keep acting.

Clothes that Speak are Clothes that Sell

So, how may a freelancer make the best of this medium? Rather simply, if you're mighty with the pen, then dollars may follow. Make cool slogans and humorous sayings and put them on tee shirts, stickers, mugs, and so forth. You may be the creator of the next big fad Tee. Think of the motto, "Shy*t Happens?" I think this was made popular in the flower child seventies. Can you even start to guess how many bumper stickers and tee shirts were sold with this? So, squeeze your brain and produce some fantastic pop culture!

T-shirts come in an assortment of styles and colors. Are you targeting a female audience? You may consider one of the many tee shirts made for women--the baby doll, tank, spaghetti straps, and so forth. Consider the color of the shirt. While colors are attention-getting, they may also clash or overwhelm out one another. Make certain the colors you choose-- for the T-shirt itself, any printed message and the colors in any graphic --will work together to produce your canvas. You want your shirt color to complement or contrast with the design. Remember that pinkish letters might not show up well on a pinkish shirt-- if the two pinks are too alike.

Have something to "state" to the world. An effective message states it in a memorable way. Think about slogans that have survived the ages, easy word combinations that most everybody has heard. As the tee shirt designer, it's your job to produce new slogans, adages or attention-getting phrases. Short is commonly better as it's more easily remembered. But, even a longer message may be memorable if it flows and has rhythm or rhyme.

Try out different fonts. When picking out a font, remember that legibility counts. But so does visual aspect. Pick a font that adds a layer of depth to your message. If the message is, for instance, "Work drives me mad," then the font may be scribbled or crazy-looking, and yet still legible. Ideally, you'll make your design in a graphics program (like Photoshop) and then use your image atone of the sites.

Say No to Shark Lenders!

Consider the art. Draw/design the art to express feelings. Which emotion do you want to conjure up? Distinguish the elements in the image that naturally arouse the desired response and then accent those elements. Are you seeking to make a sense of beauty or fright in those who see your design? The key is to comprehend the pieces of the artwork and build on them.

Place the art and text so that one doesn't distract from the other. Art may be behind the text--if the art itself isn't too busy. Art may be above or below the text. This works particularly well with oblong-shaped art so that the art basically underlines or sits above the line of text. Your art may also run along the side of the tee shirt, even crossing from front to back.

Scan and import your art images onto your file if you're using Photoshop or a like application. Incorporating art may enhance your message. Or utilize art by itself if the visual is the message you want to convey.

Come up with a Paper and Sell Ad Spaces

An illustration: In my city, there's a really prominent land agent. In all my years I had never seen this specific mode of advertising by an agent. He produced a "paper" about his geographic region. It's only five or six pages (11x17) and published on newspaper stock. It has all of the local activities, what's being constructed, how it will affect the biotic community, and so forth. Naturally, the paper is angled toward real estate news, but has just enough of the additional factors to draw in a loyal resident readership. In this paper, he deals ads to mortgage brokers, movers, title and loan companies, auto dealerships, and so forth. Now, when individuals go to sell their homes, who do you, believe they're going to call? Him, naturally! Because his name is before them bringing them news pertinent to their day-to-day lives week in and week out.

It's crucial for you to know everything about your paper. If you're brand new and are making cold calls, you'll be pelted with questions about your publication. If you are able to answer them right, you'll build credibility with your prospects. If you blunder and can't give solid info, you'll struggle miserably.

You must be acquainted with your rates and the size of each ad you have for sale. Ads can be sold either by the column-inch or by the pages, which are subdivided into particular sizes like Full-page, Half-page, 1/4-page, and so forth. It's crucial that you become fully-able to spot an ad and distinguish its size. Charge this information to memory.

Make a list of the business people you know. Begin making calls to set up sales. If you're new to the ad sales game, it's safe to assume that you won't have an existing book of business. That surely doesn't mean that you won't be able to begin selling. Almost everybody knows somebody who's either in management or owns a business. This is your quick market.

It's important for you to produce a sense of urgency for your prospects. Don't be pushy, though. Nobody likes to be pressured into anything. But, keep in mind that you're not selling a physical product like a car or copy machine. Your job is to sell the "concept" of advertising.

Sell from the top down. This step is exceedingly important. Regardless of your prospect's budget, show them your biggest and most expensive ad first. They might only be thinking of a small ad, however, they might not comprehend that by spending a little more money, they'll be using their ad dollars more wisely.

Become a master at follow through. You'll find, after your first couple of months, that the bulk of your sales will happen as a result

Say No to Shark Lenders!
of follow up. Even seasoned pros don't make sales during first attempts. You should do a follow-up no later than 3 to 5 days after your first contact. After eight or ten unsuccessful tries to close a prospect, move on to another buyer. Your time is too valuable to waste on those who are not ready to purchase.

CHAPTER 4- EARN CASH SELLING YOUR TALENTS TO SOMEONE ELSE

Tech savvy individuals can earn money online right from the comfort of their own home by setting up websites for hapless individuals who want nothing more than to have their website but have absolutely no technical skills whatsoever. Many people would love nothing better than to have a website in which to sell products or even voice political or social views. There are many reasons why individuals want websites, not all of them have to do with business and selling. However, most individuals are willing to pay someone to set up a website for them.

Someone with the knowledge of the computer skills needed to not only design a full functioning website but also knows how to register the domain name and get a server can really make a lot of money advertising their services both online and on free ad lists such as Craig's List. In addition to charging to set up the website, an individual can charge clients a fee for maintaining and hosting the

Say No to Shark Lenders!

website. There is really no end to making money at home on the internet for anyone who knows anything about computers.

In addition to setting up individual websites, a tech savvy independent entrepreneur can also use his or her skills to set up websites for local businesses. This may require soliciting local businesses, but once you get a few businesses to use your skills, you will be well on your way to having a booming online work from home business. You can charge business clients a bit more than you do individuals and chances are that they will need more help in maintaining the business website. A few business websites to maintain will be enough to get you started in your own online business.

Another option for a tech savvy individual with rudimentary writing skills to make money from home online is to write about technical issues for one of the many online writing sites that offer upfront money for articles about computer issues and technical advice. Use your knowledge of computers to make money for you in many different ways online, right from the comfort of your own home.

Technical writers are always in demand online. Technical writers tend to make more money than other writers online, particularly those who are experts in a certain technical field. If you consider yourself a computer expert, have the knowledge of how to set up websites and use codes to create graphics, you can make a nice living selling your services and knowledge to others online.

There is no limit as to how many people will want to use your services, particularly if you continue to educate yourself about any new technology in the computer world. Potential customers can include everyone from those in Fortune 500 companies to individual who want to sell items on EBay but do not know how to use HTML codes to make their auctions stand out. And advertising your services can be done with ease and very little expense.

One way to promote such a business is to contact people who are struggling to make a living on online auctions with poorly written and unattractive auction pages. You can contact them through e-mail and send them a sample of what their page could look like if you were designing the auction page for them.

Another way to promote your business is to take a look at some of the smaller websites online that look poorly constructed. Offer your services as an expert website designer to those individuals or businesses and give them samples of what their website could look like.

If you are selling a service, such as website design, you should have a website of your own that is state of the art where you can refer potential customers. This can give people an idea of what you can do - it is similar to a resume.

Payments to you for your services can be done through PayPal or other online escrow services. You need never even leave your home and can have a thriving career right online in your own living room!

Anyone who wants to promote a service online must use every avenue available to sell that service. Advertising is not as effective as contacting customers directly and building a rapport with them. If you can get them to take a look at your work, you can get them hooked.

As for selling your technical expertise by writing, there are hundreds of different websites online who will be glad to pay you for your knowledge, even if your writing is not perfect. Associated

Say No to Shark Lenders!

Content is one that will pay writers for technical knowledge. Get a Freelancer is another website where someone with technical knowledge can get hundreds of freelance writing jobs relating to technical issues and computer knowledge. The aforementioned are just two instances where someone can make money by writing about their technical knowledge online. The sites pay directly to an online account or to PayPal and you do not have to even leave the comfort of your home. Best of all, you can work as hard as you want and the sky is the limit as to how much you can make.

Tech savvy individuals have never to leave the house. There are many people online who will be glad to pay you for your knowledge, whether you actually do the work for them by setting up and maintaining a website, or write about different technological issues, there is a big calling for anyone with technical knowledge to share that knowledge. Those who have the knowledge can name their price and work online from the comfort of their own home, making a good living.

Write Impressive Resumes

At an ultra- low price of fifty dollars (I've been cited rates of $250 just for a resume); doing only a couple per day may add up to a very nice full-time income. Up-selling a package (e.g., cover letter and reference sheet) was commonly super easy, and customers were so thankful that this feeling alone was enough to make it worthwhile.

The hardest thing about writing a resume is figuring out what to accent. You must attract the attention of HR managers, who receive 100s of resumes daily even when they haven't advertised any positions.

Write a cover letter. This isn't a synopsis of your resume. Merely introduce yourself and state why you're the best candidate for the job.

Know what type of job is being applied for and what the qualifications are for employment.

Pick a design for the resume. You are able to search for samples that are particular to the job being applied for, although it's more crucial to have an outline that best suits the job and fill in the blanks with the personal information. The outline may include objective, work experience, qualifications and references.

Put in the resume the objective, fitting the job description. This may determine whether the person gets the 10 to 30 second reviews and if the reviewer will send your resume to the next round.

Utilize bullet points to convey info and strive to be clear and concise when writing the rest of the resume. Analyze the job qualifications and spotlight any skills that meet those requirements. It's also best to utilize action words like prepared, directed, managed, developed, supervised, implemented, coordinated and awarded. If there is a lack of experience, center on how education has prepared the person for the position for which they are applying.

Include symbols like %, $, and #. These symbols will save space, letting you include more information on the resume. A symbol like a dollar sign may also draw the HR manager's attention to a significant financial accomplishment. For instance, "directed and closed first year with two million in revenue" should be altered to "directed and closed first year with $2M in revenue."

Say No to Shark Lenders!

Spotlight strong points by putting the most relevant points first where they may be viewed quickly. Remain positive and prevent negatives like reasons for leaving an employer and history gaps in employment. These may be discussed in person if necessary.

Help Better Students' Grades by Proofreading

Ahhh, endearing, broke, despairing students. A lot of them don't have the time or, quite honestly, the skill level, to edit their own work. And, they'll gladly pay somebody to do it.

This is among the easiest markets to target as all you have to do is get hold of the Student Affairs office and ask to post a notice on the student message board. Or, you may take out an ad in the college newspaper. As well, flyers posted around the campus works well.

Commonly, if a student utilizes you once, they will always return if they're satisfied with your services. The finest part about this group? They have loudmouths and they utilize them -- to tell other pupils about your services.

Students likewise need resumes, bibliographies and graduate school essays. There are a plethora of services you are able to provide them successfully. I can tell you from personal experience that they are a good paying lot and are exceedingly nice to work with -- because they're commonly desperate and are just happy to find somebody who may work within their deadlines (think, "I required this yesterday!").

I don't suggest outright writing papers for pupils. I think it is immoral. However, proofing, editing, suggestive revisions -- these are all services that I have supplied quite successfully in the past.

Anthony Davis

Make Money Using Screenplays

There's a software system for all of this. As a full-service editorial firm, if you buy the suitable software, you are able to market to a particular group and establish yourself as a go-to service for that business.

I executed this for those who composed screenplays. I bought the software and took out an ad in an industry paper for artists (actors, professional dancers, musicians, and so on.). My first customer paid for the software package.

This was in 1992 and I think I paid about $200 for the software package. But, the beginning job I did for this type of customer netted me $300 (that I unquestionably recall!). The good thing about soliciting this type of customer is that they forever need revisal, updates, extra copies, and so on. I had a fee for all of this, naturally.

I always told customers that I'd store the latest version of their work for them free of charge. This made them feel truly secure and thankful. How come? I discovered many creative persons to be forgetful and a little unorganized. By volunteering this "free of charge" service, they knew that if ever they couldn't find the latest version or their computer went down, that all they had to do was telephone me.

This reinforced client loyalty -- and led to immeasurable sums of business over the years. The amusing part about working with creative persons is that you get to view the creative procedure in motion.

I had 2 customers who processed the same screenplay for over 3 years. They must have paid me a couple of thousand dollars over

Say No to Shark Lenders!

this time as they made alterations, sent copies to different offices, and so forth.

*Treatments: Treatments are one-page summaries of scripts passed on to studios for consideration. Oftentimes, a creative person will submit a treatment. If the studio likes the treatment, they'll petition the full (or a partial) script.

The rationality behind treatments? Easy... time. Studios are deluged and they simply can't read through everything presented. This technique gives them an estimation of what a script is about without having to plod through the entire thing. So, basically, what studios purchase is a "theme", not a full-fledged script. This is likewise why what the writer envisioned is often not what it ends up to be.

Sell Hot Topics to Local Newspapers

This will fly in the face of established soundness, but it's worked great for me for a long time. Rather than sending off a question, write a piece (e.g., mortgage fraudulence and its burden on the economy, and so forth.), research it well and propose it to daily news businesses.

I'd send the composition to no more than one place at a time and give them a deadline by which to reply. Let them know that as it's a time-sensitive composition, you'll give them "x" amount of time to reply (I commonly proposed three days) before proposing it to another business.

Sooner or later, somebody will pick the piece up if you abide by the method below.

Choose a hot topic: view the news and see what stories are creating every headline. For instance, hurricane season has arrived and the anniversary of Katrina just took place. Consider an issue around hurricanes and/or hurricane season and give it different angle (the outcomes of hurricanes for youngsters under twelve, and so on.).

Research exhaustively: Whatever subject you choose, make certain you reference two - four long-familiar sources. For instance, if you were going to author about hurricanes phone the National Weather Service and get a citation from an official there. Official news sources don't like to utilize unreferenced content; they prefer to state, "According to Tony Jones the head meteorologist at the National Weather Service . . ."

Aim for daily news providers: every day news sources are the ones who are most likely to choose this type of material because they're perpetually under the gun to keep the news recent.

Write SEO Articles

Writing SEO articles is easy and can be a profitable way to make money working online from the comfort of your own home. SEO stands for "Search Engine Optimized" and requires an individual to use a certain amount of keywords in the articles that are written for other individuals. SEO articles are generally short, one page articles that require a certain density of keywords. The keywords are usually given to the author prior to writing the article and it is up to the writer to do any research and incorporate the key words into the article.

There are many different online website producers who will pay money for SEO articles written by writers. Writers who want to write SEO articles for a living online should understand a little

Say No to Shark Lenders!

about keywords and keyword density and be well versed in the topics on which they are writing. It is important for the information contained in the articles to be accurate and for the articles to contain good grammar and no spelling errors. Fortunately, most people with word processing programs have spell check built right into the program. However, writers should take some time to proofread what they are writing to eliminate any glaring errors.

SEO articles do not pay much for a writer, however, there are many websites where a writer can pick up jobs to write SEO articles for money and most of them pay directly into the PayPal account or other online escrow account. Safeguards are in place for most writers as well as clients who hire the writers to make sure that no one cheats another person in the business transaction. One of the safeguards used on one popular site is the escrow system. The website owner who hires the freelance writer to create an SEO article puts the money in an escrow account in good faith. After the articles are accepted, the money is released to the writer. This works well for both the writer and the client.

Where are SEO articles used? On websites as content fillers.

Many people would rather spend their time creating websites and generating ads as well as becoming affiliates than by writing articles. Writing articles takes time, certain skills and, in many cases, research. It is often cheaper and much more time effective for a website owner to pay a ghostwriter a few bucks for a SEO article that can be used on his or her website to generate ads. This way, the website owner can concentrate on creating more websites, generating more ads and not having to bother about writing content.

Writers who want nothing better than to make a career at being a freelance writer often get a start by writing SEO articles to pay the bills. Although this may not be the creative writing for which they long, or significant political commentary, it is very helpful when it comes time to pay the bills and is the best way to make a living as a freelance writer online. If you have a knack for writing and want to learn more about writing SEO articles as a freelancer online, take a look at some of the websites that offer pay for those who do copywriting or SEO articles, such as "Get a Freelancer" and see if this is something that you would like to explore.

Write about Anything under the Sun

Suppose you want to get paid for writing online but do not want to write SEO articles or technical articles. Suppose you only want to write humor or dating stories. Can you make a living doing this online?

The answer is "possibly." It is difficult, however, unless you are an exceptional writer and have the ability to crank out at least 20 articles a day on different subjects. There are certain sites online that will pay for creative writing. You can take a look at e-zines that pay for stories, poetry and light reading articles. If you write science fiction, you are in pretty good shape. There are dozens on online publications that are seeking writers who can come up with a good science fiction story.

Erotica is another genre that pays well and where it is possible to make a living writing online from the comfort of your own home. However, erotica is not what it seems. It is more than just writing about sexual encounters. People who write erotica stories must be familiar with the genre and follow the guidelines of the online publication.

Restaurant reviews are also popular to write about online. There are a few sites online that will pay you a few bucks for writing

Say No to Shark Lenders!

restaurant reviews. However, in order to make any sort of living at this, you had better be prepared to write at least 20 reviews a day, every day.

Writing creatively online can be profitable for those who have a steady market of readers. Plenty of websites pay writers for how many page views they get on their articles. There are also sites where one can submit a story or article and sell it to others online for a small fee.

If you are planning on writing online for a living and dislike the idea of writing SEO articles, be prepared to work very hard in this very competitive field. You will experience quite a bit of rejection at first, but you must be persistent and not give up. It can take years to develop a following; however, it can be done. Once you have built up a following, you may even want to write an e-book and sell it to your readers. Just remember that there are many people online who think that they are the next Norman Mailer and you are competing with all of them.

CHAPTER 5- BLOG ABOUT WHAT YOU LOVE

Do you like to blog? Do you have a Myspace page where you reveal all of your personal information to a bunch of strangers? Do you post videos of yourself online for the amusement of your online friends? Have you built up a steady readership of people who seem to be interested in your mundane life because it reads like some sort of twisted soap opera? If this is the case, why are you wasting your time on Myspace? Get a blog on a site like Blogger.com where you can get procure Google ads that will pay you money every time someone clicks on one of the ads on your website.

Google ads are small, one line ads that are often made to look like links to other pages. They have catchy headings and can be put on personal, privately owned websites as well as some blogging websites, such as Blogger.com.

The secret to getting the ads on to your website is to first build up a readership. You can do this by making "friends" with other people who are on the site. Read their blogs, comment and invite them to visit your page. The more traffic you generate to your site, the more google will be interested in putting AdSense ads on your blog page. And the more readers you will continue to get to read your blogs.

Another secret to getting the ads onto your website and making money is to make sure that your content is relevant to the ads promoted by AdSense. If you have an obscure website about Actresses from the 1930s, you may have a difficult time getting advertisers on your site. And you will have even a more difficult time getting people to click on those ads. For this reason, it is important that your website be about something that people enjoy reading about as well as one that will pander to the many different online ads. If you are unsure about online ads, take a look at those that you see on various websites. You will see ads for health products such as medications, insurance, dating advice, dieting and pet care.

You will want to make sure that you use plenty of "keywords" in the online content for your website. It does not matter if you are a good writer when you put in your online content although you should watch your spelling and your grammar. The most important thing about your blog is that you use as many of the key words that will generate ads to your website as possible. While you do not want to saturate the content with keywords, as Google will sometimes reject such articles and they will never reach the search engines,

When you use key words in your blog writing, your blog will be picked up in the search engines for those who are looking for those keywords. Pet Insurance can be a subject to cover. You can talk about Pet insurance and use it in every paragraph. Use the phrase about 10 times in a 400 word article. You may get some google ads that pertain to pets.

In order to continue to procure readers to your blog for money site, as well as ads, you will have to continue to ad content to your blog as often as possible. The more popular the blog is with readers, the more people will begin reading the blog, responding and clicking on the different ads for pet products that will start to appear. This is how you make money blogging on the internet.

The beauty part is that you do not have to stop with one blog. If you have more than one idea, you can begin another blog and about another popular subject, such as Hollywood Celebrities. People love to read gossip about the stars or what is going on with popular TV shows. You can start a fan blog site and spend a few minutes each day blogging about the latest antics of Lindsay Lohan or Britney Spears. Use their names enough in your blogs and you will trigger ads from Google AdSense. Then, as people begin clicking on the blog, they will start clicking on your ads.

Do not depend on one website or one blog to make all of your money when blogging. I am sure that you have heard the phrase "make money blogging online." Yes, you can make money blogging online, but only if you tap into the popular markets and create many different blogs. Again, you do not have to be Charles Dickens to write a blog about Britney Spears. Just make sure you use her name enough so that the blog is search engine optimized. We will be talking about search engine optimized articles in the next chapter. All it means is that you are using enough key words for the article or blog to be picked up in the search engines. You have to be

Say No to Shark Lenders!

careful not to oversaturate the article, however, or it may end up getting rejected by the search engine.

Blogging for money can be a fun and creative way to earn money from your home while working online. It does take a bit of time to build up a readership. You can advertise your blog on forums that relate to the topic of your blog. For example, the blog about the pet insurance can be discussed on forums for people who like to talk about pets. You can join the forum and begin discussing your blog. Make a few friends and start posting your link to your blogs. Invite people on your e-mail list to visit your blogs. Leave no stone unturned when trying to generate traffic to your blog, but realize that the best way for your blog to be discovered is by utilizing key words in your content.

Chapter 6- Other Tips to Earn If You Have no Writing/Design Talents

Online Auctions

Okay, so you do not know how to write and you barely know how to turn on a computer, let alone provide technical advice. What do you do? Can you still make a living from your home by working online?

The answer is "yes." There are several things a person can do online to make money with little or no skills. One of the most popular ways to make money online is through online auctions, such as EBay.

EBay has been around for many years now and is one of the most reputable of all the online auction houses. As nearly 90 percent of people in the United States have access to the internet, online sales of products are one of the easiest ways to make money

Say No to Shark Lenders!

online. The trick to making money on EBay is to sell what people want at a discounted rate.

EBay used to consist of people selling household goods, collectibles and antiques online. While these items still make up a good portion of the stock on EBay, the most popular items to sell on this auction site are books and music. And the beauty part of the entire thing is that you do not have to even leave the comfort of your home to mail the products to the buyer or even store them.

Many online sellers, those who sell a large quantity of products online, use a drop ship method. With this method, you have no inventory in your home; nothing to store. You sell books and CDs on your auction site and when they sell, you contact your supplier and they ship the item to the buyer.

There are many ways to use the drop ship method when selling items on EBay and just as many reasons as why sellers are eager to use this service. The main reason sellers give is that they do not have to worry about storing the property. The second reason they give is that they do not have to worry about mailing the property to the buyer. They simply use their computer to manage their auctions and make sure the drop ship service knows where to mail each product. In some methods, the seller pays for the product when it is purchased. In most cases, however, the seller pays for an inventory of product that is kept at the drop ship warehouse.

If you decide to use a drop ship service when selling items on EBay, make sure that the service has a good record of mailing items to customers in a timely manner. There are forums on EBay for users and you can find out anything you want to know about particular drop shippers by asking questions.

Those who have the room to store merchandise in their home or garage can save the handling fees of the drop shippers, but will have to be responsible for the inventory. The more inventories you purchase to sell on EBay, the cheaper it is. There are many online companies that sell products wholesale to anyone who wants to buy them. While some require a state tax number for resale, most do not. You can even purchase items from other countries and sell them for a profit on EBay.

If you are planning on making a business selling on EBay, be sure that you treat it like an ordinary business. You may be working from your home, but you still need to be mindful of profits and costs for items. You must figure in postage into your sales and be sure not to underestimate postage. No matter what you are selling on EBay, you can be successful if you put enough time and effort and are a disciplined seller.

One word of caution when selling for EBay or any other online auction site - be careful of the fees. Most online auction sites charge fees for using the site to sell your items. EBay fees have risen dramatically over the past several years to discourage people from selling junk and other undesirable items. You must be certain to add the cost of these fees to the price of the items that you are selling so that you do not take a loss. Also, if you have customers who are paying through PayPal, be aware that they charge fees as well; be sure to remember those fees when listing your item on EBay for sale.

If you are a talented artist, you may be able to sell art on EBay. There are many undiscovered artists, or "outsider" artists who are successful in selling their paintings, sculptures and other artistic work on EBay. The wonderful thing about selling on this auction site is that you can reach people all over the world.

Say No to Shark Lenders!

You do not have to even leave your house to ship your items, even if you carry inventory from home. Simply use priority mail shipping from the United States post office to ship all of your packages. The post office will drop off envelopes and boxes as well as tape and labels to you free of charge and your letter carrier will take the packages from your door for delivery.

Selling items on EBay has become very profitable for some people who want to work from the comfort of their own home online but do not have any skills of which to speak to find legitimate online jobs. Although there are many other auction sites on the Internet, EBay is probably the most popular and most trusted of all. Anyone with access to a computer can sell on EBay. If you do not have a specific talent, per se, you can still make money from home working online by selling products through online auction services such as EBay.

Online Survey

Many people enjoy working from home and earning money online by completing surveys. Completing surveys online for profit is not the best way to make money online, but if you are diligent and can follow simple instructions, it can be an easy way to earn a few dollars while online.

There are many different paid survey sites online where someone can earn money from home. Be wary of those that offer to pay quite a bit of money per survey. Many of them expect you to sign up for services that will be difficult to cancel. The money you earn for the survey will not negate the money you shell out for the service, or the aggravation of trying to cancel the service.

One legitimate paid survey site is Cashcrate.com. On this website, any individual can earn money simply by following instructions and filling out forms online. The money that a person earns per survey is usually less than one dollar; however it only takes a few minutes. In order to earn money on this website, you have to be very careful to do the following:

1. Sign up for the system. This will require you to put in your name, address and telephone number as well as information that will help marketing companies send you surveys that are appropriate. Cashcrate gets their money from ads and will most likely sell your e-mail information to their affiliates. Be prepared to get unsolicited e-mails and phone calls whenever you do any surveys online.

2. Use real information. In most cases, telephone numbers are verified in order for you to get paid. The way that this survey site works is that you find a survey that you want to do and fill out the necessary information. Once the survey is complete, you have to wait for the company to verify that you are a real person and filled out the information correctly. In some cases, a call will be placed to your home via computer to verify your phone number. If you give a fake phone number, the survey will not be approved for payment.

3. Do only the free surveys listed. Unlike other survey companies, Cashcrate has a list of surveys that you do at your own pace. Some of them pay much more than others, but usually require credit card information or a trial of some service. There is an option to do only the free surveys. Use this option.

4. be wary of cell phone surveys. They will ask your cell phone number and text you that you won money if you respond. Never respond to these texts as your cell phone account will be bill sometimes up to $10. Just delete them.

Say No to Shark Lenders!

5. Only fill out the information that is required. Once you have navigated the Cashcrate website and have participated in a few surveys, you will see that the survey process never seems to end. You can continue to do the same survey for hours as you continue to be transferred to different affiliate websites. When you take a look at the survey instructions, you will see that you need only provide your name, or fill out two pages of the survey. Pay attention to this information and do only what is required in the survey.

6. Beware of offers from affiliates that will flood your e-mail box. Most of them can be helpful and are legitimate. However, most of the surveys that you will be completing are done to promote sales leads. Sales for online education, insurance, time share properties and other hard sell opportunities abound on these sites. What you are doing, by filling out the survey, is somehow telling these companies that you are interested in insurance, an online education or a time share. This will prompt a phone call from someone who will try to sell you these services. When filling out surveys, either be honest and do not say you are interested in these products, or be prepared for telephone calls from solicitors.

Some people claim to make a thousand dollars a month doing surveys online. In addition to Cashcrate, there are many other survey companies online that offer opportunities to earn a few dollars for completing questions. Most are legitimate but will only offer you surveys once in a while by e-mail. These surveys generally pay more; however, than those you do at Cashcrate.

While the idea of making a thousand dollars a month doing online surveys seems dubious, it is possible for someone to make several hundred dollars a month by completing online surveys. However, a person should be prepared for many internet offers and phone calls from solicitors. Having Caller ID and a spam e-mail inbox can help filter away these unwanted callers.

Be leery of any online website that offers to pay you cash for surveys as long as you pay a fee. While most of the sites are legitimate, there are some websites out there that offer large amounts of money for surveys as long as you join their club and pay a substantial fee. It should not cost you anything to do surveys from home. While you may not be able to pay the mortgage with the money that you make, doing surveys from home is one way to earn money online from the comfort of your own home.

Too-Good-To-Be-True Jobs Online: Should You Trust Them or Not?

Most people would like nothing better than to be able to work from home online. Imagine not having to get up early in the morning and brave inclement weather in order to go to work! There are many opportunities for individuals to work from home online, including those listed in this book. However, anyone seeking to work from home online must be careful not to fall into the trap of some of the con artists that lurk in the shadows of the internet who will offer to pay you to work online but will actually take your money.

One of the most popular scams is the "work from home typing scam." This is comparable to the stuffing envelopes from home scam that used to appear in the newspapers. Many people found it impossible to believe that anyone could make money at home stuffing envelopes. They were right. This is a long running scam that has been around for many, many years. It has only moved to the internet.

Say No to Shark Lenders!

The way that this scam works is that you will receive some sort of offer to work from home and make "thousands of dollars" a month. This should be your first tip off that it is a scam. No one is going to promise a person they do not know an opportunity to make thousands of dollars a month in an e-mail online.

You will be required to complete some sort of test that, of course, you will pass with flying colors. Once completed, you will be asked for some sort of fee for materials that you will need to begin your "career" working online typing or filling out forms. Once you turn over your hard earned money, you may get a few leads on jobs, but these are nothing that you cannot find yourself on the internet. Chances are that you will not make any money but will be stuck with a bunch of instruction booklets that will have actually cost you money.

Another popular online work from home scam is the Medical Transcriber Scam. It appears that doctors everywhere need medical transcribers as they cannot get anyone to work in their office. And medical transcribers make at least $25 an hour. The only thing they need to do is to understand the terminology used by doctors so that they can properly transcribe the information. And this is going to cost money.

The book can be prepared by virtually anyone who has access to the internet and a printer. You will get a book of medical terminology that you can easily find yourself online and a list of doctors who you can contact. The list of doctors can also be found online at the American Medical Association website. You will pay up to $100 for the privilege of getting this information that you can easily obtain for free from the internet. Be wary of the ads to become a medical transcriber and work from home online; most of them are scams.

Other popular work from home online scams involves multi-level marketing schemes such as Amway or other, less well known products. The process begins with your agreement to sell a product or service in exchange for a commission. However, you are not really selling the product, but the opportunity to also sell the product. Whoever gets you into this business will earn a percentage of everything you sell, as will the person who got them in and so forth up the ladder. By the time the product is actually sold to the individual customer, it is quite costly and undesirable for consumers. This is why the products are not sold in the stores and they need you to push the products on unsuspecting individuals as well as take full advantage of family and friends.

The multi-level marketing scam works on the internet pretty much the same way as it does on the street with one hitch - now you have to pay for the privilege of having a website that will list the products you have for sale. The website will look very professional and will be something you can show potential sellers. Do not expect to generate traffic to your website to sell your products as no one will want to purchase these products unless they feel obligated in some way.

Multi-level marketing plans are scams. They are completely legal and brilliant marketing strategies but about 99 percent of the people who sign up for such "opportunities" end up disgusted and feeling cheated. Most people do not have the heart to get their 94 year old aunt to cough up $30 for vitamins that she can get at the drugstore for $5. Or the total lack of scruples of talking someone who is out of work and desperate for money into doing what you are doing because you have become so very successful and get them to borrow the startup costs from a college education fund they have set aside for their child.

Say No to Shark Lenders!
For those whose ambition knows no bounds, however, a multi-level marketing scam, no matter what the product, can be a great ticket to success. It takes dogged persistence, very, very thick skin and the desire to dismiss any loyalty that you may have towards family, friends, fellow church members or even your own mother.

Most people need to be wary of these types of scams when seeking to work from home online. There are others that also promise the moon but end up costing you money and wasting your time. Remember that if an opportunity seems too good to be true, it probably is.

Even those with skills that they hope to sell online must be wary of the many scams that are continually generated over the internet to bilk people out of hard earned money.

Chapter 7 - Habits to Form to Telecommute Successfully

Discipline

Most people like the idea of working from home online. They imagine having all of the free time that you want, doing whatever you want without a boss looking over your shoulder and being able to watch television if you feel like it. Working from home online is just like working for a company with one big exception - you are the only one who can keep yourself in line.

Many people lack the self-discipline it takes to be able to work from home online. Instead of viewing their online career as a job, they treat it like a hobby and act accordingly. They have no set schedule; they work whenever they feel like working and generally spend a good part of the day wasting time. Then they wonder why they are not making any money.

Working from home online should be treated just like any other job. You have a starting time, certain amount of hours that you need to work, break time, lunch time and quitting time. You have to treat your online career just as it was a job. Yes, there are many bonuses. You can be flexible in your schedule if you need be. You can stay in your pajamas all day. But you have to realize that time is money, particularly when you are working for yourself. You cannot be wasting your time online messing around on websites or playing games. When you are working online from home, you have to set a certain number of hours each day to work.

When your friends and family learn that you are working from home, they will frequently call you during the day to chat or ask you to drive them places or even go shopping. Chances are that these people would never ask you to take time off work if you worked outside the home to go shopping, nor would they call you up at work just to chat. One of the most difficult aspects of working from home is dealing with well-meaning family and friends who do not understand the fact that you have to work from home online to make a living and cannot be spending your day talking to them on the phone.

One way to eliminate well-meaning intrusions from family and friends is to gently tell them that you are busy working and cannot talk. This takes quite a bit of discipline on your part as, chances are, you will be happy to hear from family and friends, particularly if you are at home all the time working online and not speaking to anyone. However, in order to get things done, you will have to limit all of your conversations to no more than five minutes. This will give you plenty of time to talk for a few minutes and then explain gently that you have a deadline and can call that person back later that day.

Another way to eliminate the phone intrusion is to use your Caller ID. Many people are slaves to their phones and pick it up whenever it rings automatically. With the advent of Caller ID, there is no need to do this. You can screen calls and only pick up the ones from those you know. Friends and relatives who understand that you are doing this should have a special code if they need to get in touch with you for an emergency - such as ring once, hang up and then call again. This will alert you to respond to that particular phone call. If you have children at school, you will be able to see if the school nurse or principal calls concerning a problem at school.

Keep the television off while you are working from home online. Most people do not have the television on in their office when they are working and you should not have the television on when you are working from home online. Television is very distracting and unless it is part of your online job, should be eliminated. Save television time for when you are relaxing. If you dislike the silence in the house and miss the noisy bustle of an office, you can play music. Some people, however, find that they are more productive when working from home online than they could be in an office because they are not hearing gossip or being intruded upon by co-workers all of the time.

Make sure you have a set schedule. This is important and will help you become disciplined, particularly when you first start your online work from home business. Begin work at a certain time and quit at a certain time. Try to figure out how many hours you will need to work each day to accomplish your goals. Your goals of how much work you need to accomplish to make your online career work should be determined before you begin your online business and should be feasible.

Say No to Shark Lenders!

Anyone who works from home needs discipline, especially those who work from home online. The internet is a fun place to visit and can be very addictive. Make sure that you are disciplined enough to make each day productive when working from home online in order to insure success in your online career.

Manage Your Time

Those thinking of working from home online should invest in a book or a seminar about time management skills. Just because you are working from home is no reason to begin slacking off during the day and becoming idle. If you continue to do this, you will not make any money and your online business will not be successful. Time management skills will help you make the best use of your time. Time management skills are often used to train individuals who work on their home so that they are more productive.

Working from home online can be a wonderful way to earn a living but it not without pitfalls. One of the major pitfalls is that most people, particularly those who are used to working for other people in an office environment, are unable to manage their time in an effective manner. The first week that they are working from home online they get sidetracked by dozens of different things and end up wasting a lot of time. Time that they should spend working. By learning basic time management skills, a person who works from home online can better manage their day and become more productive in their at home business.

Time management skills involve making each moment count. If you can get someone else to do something for you, have them do it. This can be as simple as paying a neighbor a few bucks to drive your child to school instead of driving him or her yourself each day. If your neighbor is going to the school anyway, it makes more sense for you to allow them to pick up your child so that you can spend that time working. Even if the school is 5 minutes away, chances are that by the time you get out to your car, pick your child up and come home, 20 minutes have passed. That adds up to 40 minutes per day and four hours a week. You can do a lot more with four hours a week than go back and forth to the school.

One of the basic principles of time management skills is teaching individuals who work on their own that their time is valuable. Many people do not put a proper value on their time, yet, when you ask people if they would rather have more time or money, in most cases it is a tossup. We tend to overextend ourselves with many different activities and many of them are time wasting.

In order to be an effective time manager, you have to first realize that any time you spend has worth - particularly now that you are working for yourself. It is important for anyone who wants to work from home online to understand and follow basic time management skills in order to be successful in their pursuits.

Track Your Expenses

If you are starting your own business working from home online, you will have to make sure that you keep track of all of your expenses as well as your profits so that you can declare them on your income taxes. Many companies will pay individual contractors in cash and others will require a contractor to complete a 1099 form. If you complete a 1099 form, you will have to declare the earnings that you make for that company on your income tax statement each year. In order to avoid paying large amounts of income tax for money that you make, you should be sure to keep receipts of any business expenses you incur to offset your earnings.

The IRS allows those who start up their own business to take a loss on their business for several years before it turns a profit. This can

Say No to Shark Lenders!

be beneficial to anyone who is just starting a work from home online business. By filing a loss on your business, you can deduct the money from your income tax and avoid paying too much tax.

Keep a record of all of your business transactions when working from home online. Make sure you realize your profit margin and your expenditures. Keep all receipts. This will be important when it comes time to file your tax returns.

It is also important for anyone working from home online to understand how much profit they are making, particularly if they are selling services or products online. Any fees to sell the product must be built into the sale of the product as well as any shipping costs. It is important for you to understand exactly how much profit you can be expected to make on each item that you sell.

For example, if you are like Jane, you must count not only the cost of the EBay listing and sales percentage in figuring out the price for your doggie items, but how much, exactly, it costs you to make the items. The cost of materials and supplies. This may take quite a bit of figuring, but it is important to understand if you are going to make a profit in any online business. Also, you must figure in your time. How much is your time worth? You should be getting at least minimum wage for any time spent working on a product that you plan to sell online.

You do not have to be a mathematician in order to successful account for your own business expenses and profits. You need only be able to add and subtract figures and realize that the sales price less any expenditure equals the profit. Then you have to figure out whether the profit is worth it and adjust the sales price accordingly.

This works even if you are selling non-tangible items, such as your time, online. If you are writing SEO articles, for example, figure out how long it takes you to write an article and how much you can expect to earn. The only expenditure you will have is your time. If you find that you can write three articles at the sum of $4 each in an hour, the time you invest in writing SEO articles may be well worth it. As you continue to write such articles, you can learn to maybe write four articles in an hour and earn even more money.

Working from home online has many benefits and is quickly becoming a viable option for many individuals. The advantages of working from home online include the power of being your own boss and being in charge of your own financial destiny as well as being able to use your time as you see fit. If you are disciplined, know time management skills and basic accounting, there are very few disadvantages to working from home online. The only one that some people mention is that they do not have the opportunity to meet with other people as often as they would like. This can easily be alleviated, however, by taking some time each week to join clubs. This way, you can interact with other individuals who share some of your same interests. You should also make sure that you spend a certain amount of time each week for yourself and do not overdo working. While some people tend to spend too little time working from home online, others reach to the other end of the spectrum and spend all of their time working. While this may be financially beneficial, it will not be mentally healthy in the long run.

In the future, working from home online will most likely be the norm for society, particularly for those who work in offices. For now, there are many opportunities for individuals to find a career to work from home online and these opportunities are increasing every day. In order to truly be your own boss and be in charge of your own destiny, consider a career working from home online.

CHAPTER 8- OTHER MEANS TO EARN WITHOUT BORROWING

Host a Firesale

If you've been involved in Internet business for several years, you've probably seen your fair share of firesales. Some companies do it before going out of business; while others do it as a part of their normal sales cycle. If you're in a bind and need some cash fast, then holding a firesale is probably one of your best options. Of course, if it were easy or obvious how to do this, then everyone would do it successfully; and there would be no need for a guide such as this one. But this isn't the case. Here's what I personally suggest you do to ensure that your firesale is successful:

Step #1: Pick a Demographic Before You Start

Before you even begin, it's a good idea to pick a demographic to sell to. If you don't know who your target audience is before you get started, then it will be impossible for you to select the right things to sell to them; and it will also be impossible for you to pitch to them in a relatable way.

Step #2: Develop a Truly Attractive Firesale Package

If you currently have a large product line, then this stage shouldn't be terribly challenging for you. All you'll have to do is select a handful of your products, bundle them together, and then sell them for a fraction of the normal cost. On the other hand, if you don't have your own product line, then this part could be a little more challenging. You'll have to actively seek out products that offer some type of resale license, bundle them together, and then sell them at a tiny fraction of the normal combined price.

Step #3: Compute the Savings

Once you've assembled a large package of goods and have selected the firesale price, spend some time to determine how much it would cost an individual buyer to assemble all of these products (with normal—not resale—licenses). You can then present this figure repeatedly in all of your advertisements.

Step #4: Pitch Your Firesale

Again, if you have your own product line, website, and autoresponder list, then this step will be relatively easier. In this case, you should start by pitching your firesale to your existing customers. As an added incentive, you might offer to make it even cheaper for people on your email list. A good place to start is by creating a sales page for your firesale. Be careful to detail exactly how much buyers will save, so that they understand exactly how

Say No to Shark Lenders!

good the deal is. Also, include full descriptions of every product they will have access to after buying. If you don't feel comfortable writing copy, that's perfectly fine. You can always hire someone from Elance to write the copy for you. Alternatively, you can spend some time on copywriting forums; and look for people who are marketing their services there. These individuals are more likely to have a strong background in marketing principles and copy-writing in particular (whereas those on Elance may be good writers, but not know much about marketing). Once you have a sales letter, your next step should be to make a pitch to your email list. This will require you to write some short email copy. Here, you will just want to be brief, avoid the appearance of spam, and keep the tone of a letter. A good approach is usually to say something like the following:

=============

[Name],

I don't usually do this, but I'm holding a firesale this week. I'm going to sell my entire line of products for a mere 10% of the normal price. The catch is that I'm only going to allow people to buy at this price on Friday. If you want a chance to get in on this incredible deal, I suggest that you check out what I'm offering at [firesale URL] and make sure to come back on Friday.

I guarantee you won't be disappointed.

Yours,

[Name]

=============

Again, the idea is to avoid something that appears too overtly salesy. Instead, you want to pitch it casually as an opportunity, but with a time limit and an associated sense of urgency.

On the other hand, if you don't already have a list and a line of products of your own, it's still a good idea to start by creating a sales letter; however, your approach here should probably be different. One good way to create a firesale sales letter for products that are not your own is to setup countdown clock on the page; and then incrementally add the items that will be part of your sale over time. For instance, on day one, you could add three pieces of software that will be included in the firesale to the page. On day two, you could add a bundle of 200 ghostwritten articles that will be included. And so on.

The goal of this exercise should be to get people in the habit of returning to your site daily, so that your firesale successfully builds anticipation until the final night, when your sale will begin. By this time, if you did a good job, hundreds of people will have seen your sale; and will be ready to buy. As far as the actual promotional process goes, you have several options if you don't already have a mailing list:

1. AdWords. Since your goal is to raise money fast and since the firesale will only be available for a limited window of time, AdWords is probably one of your best options when it comes to marketing. Remember to use multiple campaigns, to carefully write your text ads, and to limit each campaign to narrowly-focused set of keywords and keyphrases.

2. Joint Ventures. Find other business owners who have large, active lists. Offer them a very high commission if they participate (i.e. on the other of 50% or 75% of each sale). This will not only

help you from the sales that they bring in directly, but it will help you indirectly by raising your status by association.

3. Post on Forums. While most forums will prohibit you from directly marketing your products through a thread, most will allow you to include a signature that markets your products. You can do this in all large, relevant forums that you frequent; and when you do, make sure that you include the date of the firesale in your signature, so that forum members gain a sense of urgency.

Summary

A firesale can be one of the easiest ways to make money fast online; however, if you don't manage it correctly, you could find yourself spending hundreds of dollars on products without any real return to speak of.

Sign a Contract for a Joint Venture

If you don't already have a site and an email list of your own, a joint venture can be one of the best ways to make money quickly. When it comes to joint venture partnerships, there are three things to keep in mind:

1. Most good JV partners will reject you initially. If a person immediately accepts your JV offer, there's a good chance that she is not receiving many offers. On the other hand, if she doesn't respond initially or tells you that she'll need more time or a better offer, this probably (but doesn't always) mean that a lot of people are pursuing her as a JV partner. Why is this important to understand? Because you will get rejected many times initially when you first begin sending out offers. It is important to understand that partnerships can often be a numbers game; and that you shouldn't be discouraged too easily.

2. be courteous and make a generous offer. Often, the simple presence of a JV partner will boost your sales and your profile as a marketer far beyond what it will do for you in direct sales from that partner. For this reason, it is always a good idea to approach JV partners with a generous offer; and to be patient, kind, and courteous.

3. Stay focused in your presentation. If you're looking for a JV partner who can drive traffic to your site; and you are willing to offer a profit-sharing arrangement in exchange, then say that upfront. Make sure they understand exactly what it is that you need from them; and exactly what they will get for participating.

If you do these three things—and if you remain persistent—you have a good chance of finding at least a few JV partners who will be willing to work with you and promote your project.

Chop Up Your Business and Sell the Unprofitable Parts

If you already have an Internet-based business, but parts of it aren't performing particularly well, then it may be a good idea to sell off the unprofitable parts, consolidate everything that is working; and move forward with a new model. These unprofitable sections of your business might include websites that are poorly monetized; or products that don't seem to sell very well. Whatever the case may be, consider selling it on a forum like SitePoint.

Monthly revenue data (from AdSense or PayPal records) this will be helpful. Even if the site doesn't sell well for you, that doesn't mean it can't for someone else. This is something that is important to highlight when making the sale. Point out the positives about the site (such as its daily unique visitor counts); and then mention how this can potentially make more money if monetized better.

Say No to Shark Lenders!
One good thing about selling your unprofitable sites is that you can usually get something like 7-10 months' worth of profit from the sale. Even if your site was making a meager $100/mo., this could translate into an immediate sale for $700- 1000.

As far as e-books, reports, and unprofitable intellectual property go, consider selling them on forums. Do whatever you need to in order to make the most from them—whether it is selling the master resale rights; or simply selling to many people with a restrictive license.

ABOUT THE AUTHOR

Anthony Davis is an internationally acclaimed authority in financial planning. He was born in Minnesota but grew up in Philadelphia, where he received his degree in Economics.

From an early age, Anthony has demonstrated great interest in business. He would spend his weekends and summers helping in their bakery, where he would do the books.

www.ingramcontent.com/pod-product-compliance
Lightning Source LLC
Chambersburg PA
CBHW051239170526
45165CB00004B/1495